Nine Days

Nine Days

poems remembering Pope John Paul II

Catherine A. Hamilton

Kinglet Press
Portland, Oregon

2015 Kinglet Press trade paperback – First Edition

Kinglet Press is the imprint and ™ of Kinglet Books –
eBooks and trade paperbacks.
For information about permission to reproduce selections
from this book, write to Permissions, Kinglet Press,
4804 NW Bethany Blvd. Ste. I-2 #107, Portland, OR 97229
www.kingletpress.com

Text for this book is designed by ALL Publications
Composed by Jennifer Omner

Original photographs by Fotografia Felici,
www.fotografiafelici.com
Cover design by Michael Hamilton

Library of Congress Control Number: 2015914069
ISBN: 978-0-9967217-0-7 (paperback)
ISBN: 978-0-9967217-1-4 (eBook Kindle file)

www.catherineahamilton.com

for Greg

Contents

Days Between

Before and After

Endings

Nine Days

When the Pope Dies

It's Saturday at 12:30 in the afternoon on the second of April.
Leaving open the French doors, I wander outside
to watch the wisteria bloom nonchalantly along the arbor.
There's a green swallow circling the birdhouse
above our bedroom window,
conspiring to nest there again this spring,
aloof, thriving on other winged things.

Now from the doorway comes the sound of applause,
loud from the TV, from Saint Peter's Square.
I run indoors. I surrender to television,
to clapping—ceaseless, uproarious waves—
until the cobblestone inclines the pilgrims to quiet.
On their knees, nuns in the blue and white habit
pray the rosary when the pope dies.

Everyone knows this kind of thing happens only in Rome.
Only for the two hundred sixty-fourth pope
teenagers are crying.
The crowd is shouting—
Giovanni Paolo Magnifico! Santo Immediato!
Cathedral bells in Paris toll eighty-four times.
In Poland they sing sacred hymns a capella.

    April 2, 2005

Novemdiales

Words

Dear brothers and sisters, at 9:37 this evening
our most beloved Holy Father John Paul II returned
to the house of the Father, Archbishop Leonardo Sandri said.

But Reverend Archbishop, we don't know how
on earth to live without him.

Incomprehensible. As real as it may be,
it seems close to impossible

because it's something that many of us have never done before.
We are drowning in words deemed newsworthy,

searching for something infinitely good,
looking for his face on the front page of the newspaper. Headlines

have this feeling of disbelief,
collective loneliness.

Wholeheartedly they intend to say something
of meaning, to capture what has happened here.

We don't want to hear it over and over again,
yet we can't stop listening.

Alone I count the pebbles on the shore,
reading between the lines.

I watch the words trickle down from the radio tower,
out of the mouths of TV reporters,

some of whom simply say that words fail them
when they try to epitaph the late pope.

Pens are empty of ink
but a journalist can't find anything else to do.

"Frozen, blocked and tongue-tied…"
was what one man wrote.

I find myself wondering where the words are going,
what are they trying to say?

They try mightily to convince me they have a purpose,
that they're more than the poet's way of letting go slowly

of the only pope I've ever known and loved.
The voice of a prophet has a word of advice:

"Stand by the road and look, ask for ancient paths,
where the good way is; and walk in it."

"But I'm writing a novel," I reply.
Does it take that much faith to believe

that characters in a novel will wait on the page
where you've abandoned them?

I find the path of old and follow it;
and the words find a place to rest.

Cosmic

For those who follow a star, by definition,
for philosophers and mystics and magi,
for ghosts.
Even now, two thousand years later,
we grasp at the Real,
the Divine.
What was this once?
Dust beneath a millstone, you say.
For this homage his knees were spent
perfectly.
Longer than the last year of this pontificate
his eyes turned ever closer to heaven.
There was that moment when he passed from life
to Reality.
And we believe
our world will never be the same
because of a godstar incarnate,
because of the three kingly men,
because of gold, frankincense and myrrh
Herod will never know how to find Him.

Traffic in Rome

All night long my waking body
can't deny that it's alive.
And the alarm clock doesn't seem to mind
being left alone on the nightstand.

I look at the hour hand for the hundredth time
and add on nine, to calculate the time in Rome.

Everyone is there except my pope.
So who will be my Papa now that he's gone?

It is four o'clock this benevolent morning without sleep,
which means it's one in the afternoon at the Vatican.
I don't think my heart knows
how to consider the possibility of stepping aside

or the gravity of forever
or of that eclipse where time stands still.
It is merely a shift in the dimension
of his existence.
Especially when I see him standing
in the hallway holding his breviary.

I suppose that's not the only reason
why we don't know the day or the hour.

The sound of the traffic in Rome
is only my imagination in this darkened room
where make-believe cars can't even honk
or get a word in edgewise.

As I look at the sliver of light
that has now wandered in quietly,
stopping to ponder on the windowsill
while I wait,

you seem very close, Papa.
Is it because I hear that familiar voice,
the smile, the thoughts bearing white horses
and votive candles?

For a split second I think I understand
what you're trying to say—
that the whole of paradise is greater
than the sum of anything Italian.

St. Peter's Square

If I were in St. Peter's Square,
I'd be six thousand miles closer
to the bier of the late Pope John Paul II,
waiting in the serpentine line
that is winding its way
up Via della Conciliazione
from the basilica
back to the Fiume Tevere
and beyond for miles.

I'd be standing there beside a lady from Spain
or perhaps a fellow from London,
a Polish nun or that priest from Africa.

And if I were standing there
when they carried my late great pope
from Clementine Hall
through the bronze doors
and out into the square,
I would see more than I can see now
in the morning paper:

this still life
of twelve pallbearers
wearing gray tails
white gloves
and black leather shoes
that are undoubtedly made in Italy.

If only I could be there
when they lay him in the tomb,
at the very least, for the funeral.

But if I were there, I'd miss my mother's birthday.
She turns eighty-three this weekend,
and I want to take her the chocolate cake
that I've ordered from the bakery.
If only I could be two places at one time.

Wasn't it my mother who used to say
"If wishes were horses then beggars would ride"?

Pilgrims

It's midnight (or nine in the morning,
depending on where you live).
Yesterday they caught you wearing two watches.
You couldn't explain why, except to say
that math has never been your strong suit.

You're not the only one caught up
in the passing of a pope.
There are 1.1 billion Catholics,
and who knows how many non-Catholics,
on virtual pilgrimage to the Vatican.

Seriously you consider getting out of bed
to watch the television,
knowing the basilica is now open.
Instead you reach for a pen and paper
to jot down a few notes,
rattling at the nightstand drawer,
disturbing your husband's sleep.

Quietly now you whisper prayers for the pilgrims.
Some won't get in to see him.
Some fainted waiting.
All roads lead to Rome—
that's what you've always heard.
But there was such a crowd on Monday
that the trucks couldn't get into the city with food.

What if every street-corner café has closed?
Drifting off to sleep you dream
they airdrop bundles of cheese panini to the hungry pilgrims.

The White Miter

There are one hundred thousand pilgrims
gathered in St. Peter's Square;
do you really want to be one of them?

Absolutely. No question about that.

But you settle for the next best thing: the computer screen,
where there's this picture of the Holy Father
lying in state at Clementine Hall.
The shepherd's staff is tucked under his left arm.

You have a closer look—
the white miter is one you haven't seen before.

Do you think the red satin fabric of his chasuble
will last forever? What about the pallium with
the nails of Christ that covers his white papal robe?

Without a doubt,
something beyond infinity.

A rosary in his hand,
in front of the camera and the world,
even now, even in death,
he seems larger than life,
having lived out each mystery to the end,
remembering every saint,
some of whom the rest of us have forgotten.

Less prepared for the totality of things
than is optimal, you print a copy of this picture.
How long will you save all these photographs of Karol Wojtyla?

You don't know.

There's the stack of journals on the desk,
and a shelf full of books about him,
not to mention the five-inch-thick folder of his encyclicals.
You haven't read every word...nothing to be embarrassed about.
Time *is,* after all, a limiting factor.

How long, you ask, does a person feel this sadness,
this heaviness? They say it will pass,
but do you believe them?

One can always hope...

You would never have guessed
that when it was one o'clock in the afternoon in Rome
you'd be skulking about in the dark
worrying about the poems
and the two doves that have made a nest
below your bedroom window.

They are sitting on the three eggs
that are haphazardly nestled in the mossy
branches of the cherry tree.

The roost is exposed
because the tree hasn't any leaves yet.
For some unknown reason
that doesn't seem to bother the two of them.

One dove sat on the nest through a rainstorm yesterday
with its eyes closed,
trusting the weather would be fair tomorrow.

But just now you forget about ornithology.
You turn on the television and watch
the College of Cardinals convene in Rome.

By Chance

He lived in Thailand when the tsunami hit;
it took every last speck of the beach town
he once called home.

Survivors sift through memories
by chance to find a tablet of paper,
a missalette,
a page to write upon,
tattered and wrinkled
but still recognizable.

Now he lives in Rome.

There are touch relics,
paper cups trampled underfoot,
a baby bottle miraculously unbroken.
Those who are in Rome, he says,
know what the obelisk points to.

He's a shopkeeper now.

He sweeps the sidewalk,
saving bits of sand, hiding the suffering
in his pocket.

He tries to pick up the pieces.
He sighs deeply and says aloud,
"I'm gonna miss him."

Zinc and Wood

It's cold.
I wrap my shoulders in a heavy chenille throw
and my mind around a series of poems by Karol Wojtyla:
MEDITATIONS ON DEATH.
I devour his words and a Bartlett pear.
The dog whines for a scrap of lunch.
There is talk of autumn here.
You turn to dust, he wrote.
How old was the poet then? They are undated.
Twenty-one? Thirty-three? Forty-eight like I am?
How long was he *deathbound,* moving towards mystery?
Now the dog is crying for a bowl of water.
Waves of sadness drip from the shawl
covering my existence.
I am drenched.
"Fear Which is at the Beginning" is my favorite.
You read the poems and decide for yourself
where body and soul go.
The poet's Funeral Mass is the day after tomorrow.
Then the sum total of his earthly remains,
unrepeatable atoms
will rest in zinc and wood,
and with him, a scroll, a face veil, a rosary and a small bit of dust
from Wadowice.

Memorial Mass

Even though she couldn't go to Rome,
there was a Memorial Mass at the local Cathedral.
She heard about it on the evening news,

and when the phone rang, the lady on the other end said:
"The Knights and Ladies should march in the solemn procession."

"Indeed, but we need an invitation. Who will call the Archbishop?"

While she found it strange
that daylight had dimmed significantly,

it came as no surprise to her
that the flashlight battery had drained the night before,
even though the prayers had not.

Phone calls took up most of the day.
Waiting for an answer from the chancellery,

she began to wonder
what had happened to the pearl rosary
that had traversed the Italian Alps with a bohemian bishop
who was due for his *ad limina* visit
on the occasion of the pope's eighty-fourth birthday.

He will, no doubt, do a lot of good from heaven.

In the late afternoon of said day
a call came from the bishop's office,
with an emphatic "Yes" to the Equestrians.

The Soldier and a Cherub

Down the aisle where a bride and groom,
a first communicant,
and candidates for confirmation have walked,

now come the Knights of Columbus,
the Knights of Malta,
the Equestrian Order of the Knights and Ladies
of the Holy Sepulchre of Jerusalem.

And when the church was filled to overflowing,
and every row and every seat was taken,
twenty priests and a bishop offered the Sacrifice of the Mass.

All at once the choir started singing
a Celtic alleluia.
And glory, could that choir ever sing.

Approaching infinity,
that place
often referred to as eternal bliss,

were the soldier and a cherub named Chloe.
Someone had asked them to bring the gifts to the altar.
He carried the wine and the burdens of war,

she brought bread and blond curls.
She looked like a girl from Krakow
in that flowered skirt and eyelet blouse.
Those ribbons that trailed softy from
the wreath 'round her head seemed to say:
farewell, farewell, farewell to the Polish Pope.

The Garden

Cruciferae is the Latin botanical name
for what is commonly known as candytuft.
It blooms lavish cross-like clusters
that grow beneath the old cherry tree
where the doves are nesting.
I've seen them both sitting on the eggs.
Natural law was gracious enough
to deign they take turns
with the tedious job of incubating.

Watching from a place near the front door
the tulips send salutations.
They are in awe of the world
and offer themselves completely.
Let everything in the garden be a litany of praise.
Please, every plant and tree and shrub, give alms:

the daffodils, the tulip tree, the daphne,
the camellia, the andromeda,
the grape hyacinth, the electric blue forget-me-nots
and the red tulips
that now grow where the white ones were.
The crocuses have passed on too,
but in their place a primrose holds
a lace-trimmed bouquet.

After a while, a flicker wings past my office window,
landing in one of the cypress trees
that towers over the generosity of the lowly woolly thyme.
I see the topiaried boxwood has new leaves for the occasion
and the dogwood tree, now in full bloom,
inclines toward the statue of a saint,
Francis of Assisi holding a bird.

On the arbor above the kitchen window,
the clematis opens, its petals blushing
like a choir from the balcony.
And while I'm carrying on about this color and that,
someone is at the front door.
Really I should leave my desk
because my boxer, Ciapek, is barking.

But I don't bother to go see who it is.
I just ask him to please "Be quiet."
But now he is scratching at the long lonely window
beside the door,
something he does only if the someone
who is there is the neighbor cat,
standing outside, teasing him.

It's time to get up from this garden poem
and fill the spray bottle with water.
I sneak past the dog and go outside,
around the back of my house, almost running.

I descend upon the scene and find
one of the doves hunkered down
in the cherry tree watching everything.

For the sake of the dove,
I let go a blast of water on the tabby.
The spraying sound sends her scrambling
skittishly to her own yard.

The dog sees what has happened
from the front-room window
and is now pouting.
He would rather have handled
the problem of the cat himself.

The dove hasn't moved. In fact,
it doesn't seem at all surprised
that there's a life and death struggle in the garden.

Notebook

I have myself a coffee with cream while the whispering poet
takes a nap on sheets of lilting white paper.
For sure the household needs a moment of silence,
so I stop tapping on the keyboard.

I think about reading something plentiful
besides the newspaper, taking advantage, helping myself
to the box of chocolates that hides in the far corner of the pantry,
but instead I meditate upon locutions.

Some interior things can be more worrisome than others,
like when you are bereft of a notebook
just when a poem flings itself into your lap
without a moment's notice. But even worse
when a verse up and vanishes.

It occurred to me like this: a muse can give up the ghost,
but I can't imagine that a eulogy possibly could.
Though it makes sense that all obituaries
will cease to exist in the end...while we wait.

It was during the sermon that the whisperer returned,
an endless generation of fervent trumpets,
the piping of lofty nightingales,
that is, if I heard correctly.

I fumble in my purse for the part of me that is listening
to a never-ending stream of summer days about to breach.
With stubborn carefulness, I refuse to disturb
the man sitting in the pew behind me.

Maybe he'll think I'm taking notes on the homily.
I scribble something down and it is soon etched
in the marble flooring. Thank God, it's barely legible.
I fold my hands and beg for mercy.

On Thursday

Thursday is laundry day,
and she gets up early to start a load of wash.

The Easter bouquet of pale lilies
is drooping on the sidetable, and
she hasn't the heart to throw it out.

For local artists today is Ruby Thursday.
Sixty-two red paintings will be on exhibit.
Her great-aunt Helen also does the laundry on Thursdays.

But TODAY is the Thursday of *Novemdiales*
and there are only five more days of mourning.
Her pope's funeral is tomorrow.

On Thursday she always prays the Mysteries of Light
on her amber rosary beads.
Her husband needs to take a sack lunch today.

This is one seventh of April she will never forget,
the feast of St. John Baptist de la Salle,
the last day the pilgrims will pass by the Holy Father's bier.

She forgot to stop by the bakery
to pick up her mother's birthday cake today.
But there's always tomorrow.

When her husband gets home from work,
they have a light supper and retire to the bedroom.
At 1:00 a.m. the Mass of the Resurrection is on television.

Wearing a full-length white robe,
she stands awaiting the most watched event in history;
she makes the sign of the cross when the requiem begins.

Funeral Incense

By the time they arrive,
the lid on the coffin is closed.
These kinds of things aren't easy to explain.
There is the plain cypress box,
the cross, the M (for the Virgin Mary),

the pages of the red book of gospels
turning faster and faster,
one page after the other,
in what seems like a holy gale,
until the earth and the choir have finished singing
"Grant Him Eternal Rest O Lord."

From behind the Holy Door
comes the cardinal's procession.
And now, as if from the crimson rhapsody
there is a gust of mighty wind
that makes the red and white flags
want to loose themselves from the earth
and flutter aloft with folded hands
that billow and hold skullcaps,
praying for the late Bishop of Rome.

According to Karol Wojtyla,
there is only One who can
"retrieve our bodies from the earth."
The violence and strife have now ended
and they have not had the last word.
The Holy Ghost opens and closes all things
immutably.

The Chair of Peter is vacant.

Stirring hearts grieve
while singing in Latin.
The thurible swings on a brass chain,
sweetly sending funeral incense
circling like a bird who has escaped the monocular,
up to the third-story window
to say his good-byes.

China isn't there for all the wrong reasons,
but the Oriental Rite intones a mesmerizing
plea for the forgiveness of his sins,
dousing their blessings on the coffin
with holy water and tears and condolences.

The crowd is hoping the recessional hymn will never end.
Now they are shouting: "Sainthood immediately!"

They applaud and then fall suddenly silent.

April 8, 2005

Orphans

The Crown Plaza Hotel is full, and the restaurant Barone
serves hot *bruschuetta*.

Orphans walk the streets of Rome
eating bread,

looking in their backpacks for prosciutto,
looking for Papa.

At the corner cafe sits a lone latte.

Three orphans drink cappuccinos,
but who are they?

Her skin is dark,
and his eyes are green

and that one has long blonde hair.
His name Pedro, Piotr, Piere.

And her name?
Maria, Marjo, Marie.

Life's Wonders

I especially like to walk the dog on mornings
so ordinary as this one.
Small wonder that he is happily sniffing his way
across the everyday suburban street.
Some whiff or other is always of interest—
for him it's the daily news.

Oh, I guess there *are* such a great number
of things to ponder, gifts
that unwrap themselves before my eyes
each and every day of this
most amazing life.

There are, I think, too many to name here,
and yet it seems worth trying
to list a few that come to mind.
While I leave the road where it is
and breath this air
fresh as the big-leafed magnolia,

seven things seem like a lucky number of wonders:
That geese can fly in the dark of night.
That the sage is blooming in the herb garden.
That the black-capped chickadees
        found the nesting box, even though I moved it.
That there are animals and emails and internet.
That there is such a thing as Holy Matrimony.
That life is exactly what it is.
That there are museums and monuments and music
        and green, green grass.

Sister Sobodka

Even though I don't know you, I have a question.
Could I give you a hand with the cleaning?
Maybe fold up what's left in the closet?
Are his socks in the top drawer?

How long before the papal apartment
needs vacating? And how, I wonder,
will you manage to move the flower box
from the window where the doves
lift off and land again, leaving for good,
it seems, a friend who just a month ago
was sitting in the sunroom on the third floor?

Sister Sobodka, you don't have to answer me today,
but can I sweep and mop,
dust the banister and the railing along the stairs?

Whatever might lighten the load.

Wipe down the baseboard molding?
Polish the brass lock on the door?

What I'm asking is,
is there anything, anything at all
that I can do on my knees?

I am here at home thinking
that perhaps the willow trees
in Poland will offer you comfort
if you return there,
that their keening might ease your sorrow.

You are there in Rome doing housework
with a new kind of devotion,
bearing the weight of lost hours
across the marble hallway
with the blanket that covered him
while he was dying.
Thank you, Sister, for what you've done for all of us.

The Feast of Saint Stanislaw

At Holy Mass, the priest says the entrance antiphon
for the saint, bishop and martyr.

It is still *Novemdiales.*

The one man was born in Szczepanow,
the other in Raba Wyzna.
Two martyrs: one of the flesh, one of the will.

It was early that particular morning
when the thrush and the humming bird
shared a branch in the poplar tree.

Fields of winter wheat rippled in the breeze
and the plowed landscape lay dying,
rolling beyond the foothills of the Tatras.

Apprehension grew like the grass,
and yet he rose from bed to pray
because the day was new with the light,

and because he believed in the endless days of this lifetime.
The bishop of Krakow, Stanislaw Szczepanowski,
did not fear the likes of King Boleslaus II.

Once inside the chapel of St. Michael outside the wall,
he faced the altar unwavering,
unaware that the king's guard was lurking close-by.

A grain of wheat fell into the chalice.
One could ask the question:
What good is martyrdom?

The sword was sharp and heavy,
the flesh on the back of neck, soft.
The blow hit hard, but not from the guard's swing.
It came from the hand of a murderous king.
The lance of Boleslaus dripped with blood.

One could ask the question:
What good is martyrdom?

There were hundreds of thousands baptized
after that. And to save mankind
the Sacred Liturgy is celebrated continually.

The memory of the slaying and of the blood is still fresh.
They still weep. Still, they mourn the loss of the patron of Poland.
It seems like only yesterday that he was here.

One Stanislaw was born of noble parents,
the other of humble.
Two martyrs: one of the flesh, one of the will.

With indebtedness I write this poem
for Archbishop Stanislaw Dziwisz of Raba Wyzna,
the private secretary of the late pope.
This cannot possibly be a festive day,
but it is, after all, his Name Day.

One could ask the question:
How can *Novemdiales* be over tomorrow?

Another dares to answer:
This may be the last of nine days,
but deep down the heart of grief knows
nothing of the celebrations.

Yet there is no end to the Church or to her prayers.
St. Stanislaw, pray for us.

Nine Days

Standing on the Warsaw stage
I heard him recite the lines from *Balladyna*.
It was as if he'd become the poem.
(And though I didn't actually hear his voice,
because my ears hadn't yet opened,
there are fond memories of him.)

And now I find myself wondering
about that warrior dressed in ironclad armor,
that Slavic soldier with wings
who bore the nine swords of destiny.

Although, in those days, the queen was a luminous light—
her tears fell for the innocent of this world and the next.
The string of beaded mercy that festooned her legacy
was something much more than a ritual.

By then the names were called aloud eight times.
It was her guess that when Karol Wojtyla took ahold of the throne
the miter and the crosier would consume him.

But it was Norwid who wrote his favorite verse:
For the Land where a crumb of bread
Is raised from the ground with reverence…
I yearn, O Lord.

Oh, don't cry gentle reader,
Nothing can spoil the meadow now.
See that immense crown of glory
growing like mighty gilt lilies.
Engraved are the names in volumes,
studded and bejeweled,

and to all you levelheaded,
to those wreathed in emeralds,
nine days will not be enough time to mourn,
nor to write a suitable ending for this poem.
(I should mention that today is the last day of *Novemdiales*.)

April 17, 2005

Days Between

The Vacancy

I would like to say with all solemn certainty
that it's no small wonder the vacancy threw everything
in Rome off-kilter.

Is there a better word to define such a void,
a state of being unoccupied, empty?
The absence of color in a black and white photograph

is one thing, but this is arguably another.
And who, may I ask, will pronounce *urbi et orbi*,
who will address the city and the world?

Are people ready to talk about white smoke or the toll of the bells?
I look for balance, wonder if those walls are straight up and down.

It does seem like they're leaning,
one to the right and another to the left,
caught between one conundrum and the other.
                                        Where is the center?

All morning long my fingers pass over the keyboard
searching for braille and homonyms,
for anything that might speak clearly to a puzzled heart.

At last, I can't help but think about the poor orchid in the vase
beside me. Sweet as it seems, it hasn't pages to say—
and it hasn't the vaguest idea what it's doing off the stem.

So while I'm out shopping for my mother's birthday card,
I find answers in a new white orchid.
There is this feeling of unmistakable gratitude.

Driving home I see a bumper sticker that says: Pray the Rosary.

The Lost Dove

It was when my mind carried me out to the mailbox
that I discovered the doves' nest had disappeared.
There was no sign of violence, no ruffled feathers
on awfully hard ground, not a fragment of an eggshell.

The cherry tree has a secret. But naturally, it prefers not to
talk about it. Having thrown its blossoms into oblivion,
the spring is fearless of extinction.

We guess many things, but this I know for certain:
one dove is here and the other is gone.
The one who is left looks lost, wandering across the lawn

and into the tangle of *Cruciferae*, calling
Coo-ah, coo, coo, coo, realizing a quintessential
moment has passed.

We blame the cat.
"Did it come as a surprise?" you ask.
"No. We expected it."

The moss knows something, too, but speaks only to the clouds
drifting silent and innocent over the neighborhood.
The left one has nowhere to sit down.
Nothing seems right. Nothing is right.

It takes time for a dove to mourn,
a year, maybe two. Some birds take a lifetime.
There are distractions.

Luckily flying makes one forget the pains of earth.
One recalls the love, but its memory is nothing
in comparison to the ecstasy that is aloft.

Coo-ah, coo, coo, coo.

Ocean of Mercy

They are countrywomen and men and cousins,
crimson poppies scattered across Italian marble stairs.

They are bent on seeing the son of Poland
one last time,

knowing St. Peter's door
won't return him to his homeland,

though they are much obliged to have for themselves
an Archbishop named Stanislaw Dziwisz.

And now the downpour has
fixed upon the promise of rainbows

sewn to the hem of Madame Curie's lab coat.
If only she were here

she would explain everything,
like how those mysterious rays of light

can change crystals, how they move
weightless and invisible, revealing everything.

The stairway is now quiet.
Jozef Pankiewicz and his painting of anemones

take part in the flower's family reunion,
but please see the picture of them waiting by the wayside

for the bronze portal to open.
(It's been what seems like an eternity.)

There are lines for confession
and time for people to examine their conscience.

Deep down in the grotto there is another door;
beyond the stone pillars of ancient of Rome,

beyond the cypress trees that line the catacombs,
flooding the river Tevere,

reaching the tombstones at Monte Casino,
there is an Ocean of Mercy.

Love

I know that horses can't be blue
because there is reality,
nor can a donkey be yellow like in that ethereal painting.
But sometimes I wonder where the love comes from.
From Middle-earth? from the celestial choir beyond ecstasy?
by the fact of my existence?

You wrote that Love explained everything,
resolved everything.
Tell me, love, where did you go?
If I could only see you one last time,
maybe
send a card on your birthday
or make you a bowl of pierogi or a strudel makowiec.

What once seemed improbable,
today is possible.
And yet
I am nothing without Love.
How long will you awaken me alone at night
to question these things?

Lines Like Those

I return from the bookshelf
and wait for some new version of software
to download on my computer.
I can't help but wonder,
while the PC hums mindlessly,
whether Wislawa Szymborska
came up with something clever.

Or had her first line been something serious?
Had she scribbled the first draft in pencil
or in ink?
Did the invention begin on a paper napkin
or was it hammered out on a typewriter?

Did she call him "His Holiness" or "Papa?"

Without the least bit of evidence,
I imagine that she attended his funeral,
sure that she has no fear of flying.
But maybe she doesn't like crowds,
much less traveling.
For all I know, she doesn't even watch TV.

Will she think it odd
that an unknown American
had so much to say about the Polish Pope?

(I'm of Polish descent, in case that matters.)

Suppose for the moment, if you will,
that she has written a few verses
like the ones she wrote in praise of her sister.

Lines like those win Wislawa Szymborska prizes.

I know as well as you do
that the dead can't speak for themselves,
but as one of the living, I have found
that her poems have something to say
about life and death.

That's the very reason why
I wish she were here beside me
to carry into existence this empty page.

For a fleeting moment, I think
I grasp the half of it,
think I have it pinned down at last.

But that moment has escaped me completely
and fluttered off like a butterfly
to mother the flowering rue.

Flight 100

Standing at the middle of the tarmac
for the sendoff was every red-crested cardinal on earth,
every sandpiper and golden plover,
pair after pair of grey-backed tern
dressed fastidiously in black tails and white bowties.

The white egret, the rock dove
and the everyday sparrow was there, too.
No one noticed the short-eared owl
who was wondering how to proceed.
But when the flock of black-crowned night heron arrived,
everyone erupted in a noisy chatter.

Then the white eagle
boarded LOT Flight 100 for the last time,
setting off happily, happily,
but leaving behind millions of birds,
including the ring-necked pheasant.

Already inside of infinity,
airily lifted,
eyes have their fill of aquamarine
and saints from every nation
come to greet him the instant
he disembarks

intrepid.

No baggage claim, no jet lag,
no squawking mynah bird,
no thorns on the bougainvillea.

Paradise

We are dining out on the veranda,
finishing the last glass of wine,
the last piece of pineapple dipped in chocolate.
Still lingering with us are the speckled songbirds
that beg what they can from the table,
things that would otherwise
have gone to waste
or to sparrows.

It is the end of the day,
the week, the month,
the millennium—a stupendous
temporary homeland island in paradise.
And now before us
the tropical sunset fades mightily
on a long-lived wave of fascination,

dappled headlong in shades of papaya
and of Monet blue
whose pond
is forever filled with water lilies.

To many, it seems
a primitive supplication.
But it was not that long ago
when the inhabitants here believed
in the luck of a rabbit's foot.

We were told by the locals that
a glimpse of the white owl in broad daylight,
though rare, was without a doubt,
now, and always will be,
a good omen.

We ponder the goddess Pele, who
walked these islands with her sisters
and went to live inside the highest of mountain volcanoes.
No one knows whether her explosive temperatures
came from her father's or her mother's side.

For the time being, suffice it to say
that the lava-spewing goddess can be scary
to even the bravest of islanders—
so we are told by the brochure
that ends by saying: fear Pele no more.

We heard it as if it were only yesterday,
coming from the third-story balcony,
a sort of revival—a great awakening.
The benediction was an authentic proclamation
in the time of *anno Domini*.

May the angels accompany you on your journey
with bouquets of orchids and anthurium;
may I meet you in paradise under the plumeria.

Natalia

In December she looks like the angels
that winged across her canvas motionless, formidable.

Archangel-like, yes—but at the same time
cherubesque,

a creature both frightening and approachable.
Truthfully, I didn't meet her in person

but discovered that Natalia Tsarkova
is the official portraitist of Pope John Paul II.

A genius with a paint brush.
Blonde.

Sensibly dressed, she is the first Russian Orthodox
to win the favor of a Roman Pontiff.

(I do wonder whether people see her in the Piazza Barberini
having gelato.)

She paints pictures of popes and saints in basked magnificence,
also the duchess and the duke, and ordinary folk,

and horses,
and cityscapes with love, and sometimes with a sense of humor.

Upon finishing the near life-sized canvas called
"Our Lady of Light," she presented it to the Holy Father

for a private viewing the day before Christmas, in 2004.
The apocalyptic Madonna holding the Child aloft,

away from the dark clouds and phantoms of evil.
There, too, are four celestials:

Joyful, Glory, Sorrowful and Light,
urgently, fervently

they are proclaiming the Christ.
A serious work, no disagreement on that. Eschatological.

I would expect nothing less from a woman
so near to the heart of Michelangelo.

But what is this on the veritable trumpet of Glory?
I use a magnifying glass to see this detail.

It is a miniature of the pope sitting in an airplane on his way
to Moscow, a mutual dream of painter and pontiff.

A Prison

In a lawn chair, sitting a careful distance
from the swimming pool,
I play the part of the tourist.
Swimming suit, sun hat, tanning lotion,
I pretend to be like everyone else,
to be enjoying myself.

I have often tried to be satisfied by
such things,
holidays, sitcoms,
a French manicure.
Should it take this much effort?

It just so happens, and lucky for me,
that the laptop fits nicely
into the oversized swimming bag.
No one considers this a serious occupation, writing.
My father keeps asking
when I am going to go back to work.

It was there by the pool, in the scorching sun,
four days shy of spring,
that my computer froze up
in mid-sentence,
no trace of where I was,
no memory, no backup file,
no rhyme or reason.

A poem isn't that important anyway,
nothing more than lying on a beach
with sand between my toes.

It is a prison of sorts,
these lines, that road, those hills,
the verse scribbled on the crumpled pages
under the abandoned lounge chair.

It was something I had read
in a forgotten journal about the pope,
about his swimming pool at Castle Gandolfo,
that he enjoyed the water as much as he loved chocolates.

Sympathy

There was a photograph on the greeting card,
a single red rose in a glass jar.
The sender was a doctor, a Quaker,
    sincerely your friend

wanting to give you his sympathy.

Please know that we are thinking of you
and may gardens of memories bloom
in your hearts and bring you comfort.

It was much appreciated.

In a nicely handwritten note he asked
whether you had attended the pope's funeral.
The answer was no, sadly, regrettably.

You were pleased, though, that there were
so many people who did—

not only prime ministers and presidents,
kings and queens and princes,
priests, pastors, rabbanim, clerics, orthodox patriarchs,
but there were thousands upon thousands
of ordinary people from all walks of life,
too many to name them all here—
an estimated four million.

You read aloud the prayer for world peace
printed on the enclosed holy card,
and also the one for peace in Jerusalem.

Brimming

It has seemed to me for some time now
that the sun is its brightest
during that one lackadaisical moment

just before it slips behind the floating cloud
that is unmistakably
old enough to be my grandmother.

I wonder if a person's heart is truly finished loving
at the end of a lifetime
filled with unfettered smiles.

Or does it linger out there
somewhere
behind the kisses of immortality?

When it comes to things like this
it makes more sense
if I rely on the numbers leading to infinitude.

I must say, though, that I have more than once wondered
why some people drown their sorrows,
but then, what with all the saltwater brimming over

and swallowing up the dry
memories that can't be found in books,
I don't doubt there is much need of lamentation.

The Window

I watched my expensive pair of sunglasses
scud across the tabletop and fly out the window

carried by an unexpected wind
that has taken nearly everything in sight.
I squint, blinking at the smallest bit of daylight...

There is no ledge on the planet Earth
nothing to hang on to here
no strings attached
so, please—be careful.

It is true. We have survived this far. And yes,
there are still seven days in every week.
The red traffic lights still stop the cars.

Oh well, the sunglasses can be replaced, anyway.
But there is no replacing last Sunday afternoon
or next Monday morning or you.

I have not forgotten about the sun, the way
it keeps carrying me toward what seems to be an
ever-growing and insatiable need for yellow.

And then, after the long day is over, I remember
why the royal palms raise their arms,
calling the rivers to flow and the deserts
to bloom, growing miracles as if it's no secret at all.

Polish October
20 October 1956

What weapon is a date of birth?
a life? a word?

What defense is a pen?

Some people don't care
what happened yesterday.
For them there is no tomorrow.
They don't write it down,
so all is forgotten—
beginning, middle, end and eternity.

To them I write cryptic on thin air.
I hope to dilute the emptiness,
carrying them along with

the suffering dove
whom I had grown so accustom to,
and had even come to love.

Another person doesn't want to hear
about those trapped beneath the rubble.
"Forget it! Why think about them?" they say.

I answer, "If someone cannot fathom darkness,
how can someone fathom light?"

There is a distinct possibility
that my amazing mother gave birth
to me that very day for a reason.

A Very Old Poem

In case you haven't read the lines
Of this very old poem,
A verse written
By the Polish poet, Juliusz Slowacki,
Here are a few of them:

> "Amid discord God strikes
> At a bell immense,
> For the Slavic Pope,
> Open is the Throne.
> This one will not flee the sword,
> Like that Italian.
> Like God, He will bravely face the sword,
> For Him, the world is dust...
> So behold, here comes the Slavic Pope.
> A brother of the people."

In case you didn't know,
Slowacki wrote that poem in 1848.
Amazing, isn't it?
Prophetic.

The Chapel and the Ring

It was twenty-two years after his election,
during the Great Jubilee Year
when I stepped up to greet him.

I knew he liked people to feel
as if they were all on equal ground—
that he wasn't inclined to want them to
kiss the pontifical ring.

When he was installed the 264th Bishop of Rome

he refused to be crowned or call it a coronation.
And that was the reason why I didn't kiss the ring
on that day in the year 2000 AD.
That was why I let the opportunity pass me by,
but sometimes I think I'll go to my grave

regretting it.

Perhaps it was for the best, though,
knowing where he was coming from...

remembering the chapel built on a river
instead of on a parcel of land in Poland,
all because some tsar (whose name we've all
forgotten) prohibited the building of Roman churches
on Polish soil for an unimaginably long period of time.

Many pictured the floating church,
and passersby built it out of wood
one piece at a time.
Tell them dry bones that it still stands.

It was as if the limestone arches standing
in the cave-laden Ojcow forest knew
more about what it took to be Jurassic
and thought nothing of it.

The facts were the facts: the people had faith.

It's easy to believe that the descendants of this
church-building tribunal whispered something
about the wood and the rock incessantly.

For them it was natural and rather an instinct to
contemplate the meaning of it all when a brother
became the pope—a saint.

Unsent Letter

Dearest Letter:

I have accidentally misplaced you. You were handwritten in ink, in rudimentary Polish, weren't you? On personalized half-sheet letterhead, if I'm not mistaken. Yes, on 25 percent cotton paper.

You are now what you were then, an unsent letter to a pope. A little light on the subject couldn't hurt. Honestly, I can't help but ask one question: Who dares to address oneself to a pontiff? I know what you're thinking, but it's not like you could have signed the page, *yours fondly, poor unworthy daughter, Catherine of Siena.*

There are five cardboard boxes full of articles and old query letters. I carry the box made of leather to the window, where the view is exhilarating. The red-winged blackbird is flying past and into the blue sky that is usually here to help out. Other birds are content to float toward the distant sycamore tree.

Oh, at long last, I found you folded inside the notebook where dreams have written themselves into incredible realities—there you are. Your Polish wasn't good then and now is no better. To decipher the heart of the message requires the use of a Polish dictionary.

Regretfully, now that I've found you, I'm afraid there's nothing here that hasn't been said before, summed up in three words—faith, hope and charity. It is too bad, though, that someone didn't send you.

Sincerely yours,
Unsigned

P.S. For sentimental reasons, I'll keep you in the folder labeled: When a Saint Comes to Visit.

First Conclave

On the third Sunday after the pope died,
the choir sings a Polynesian hymn
on this island where we've come to rest.
Their eyes close as they enter the deep.
Have their hearts slipped away,
searching like mine for the place they've laid him?
O Death!
That final hour we will not forget forever.
Now is the time to be left behind, counting the days,
waiting for my smile to return from the crypt in Rome,
from the floral laden tomb.
O Life!
Leave the wren in the bougainvillea,
leave the song and live out your days,
holding onto poetry like pain, like a burnt offering.
I cry for my Polish ancestors.
O Paradise!
The Slavic Pope has come and gone.
Tomorrow the cardinals will hold the first conclave.
There is a flaming tree here called dazzling hope;
it doesn't have a vote, but it believes in something.
O Eternal City!

Seventeen Days

The days skulk past like relatives
wandering in the graveyard,
looking for names they might recognize.

They count the number of verses
that attend them during this time of waiting.
There are fifty-one.

They had hoped to find eighty-four,
one for each year of his life,
but they can't control the arrangement

of headstones or the broken pencils
and try to accept that fact.
Is the telephone ringing?

They are out of breath but answer anyway,
and a sister says: "Do you see white smoke!"
They listen to the bells through the receiver.

No time for good-byes now because in Rome
everyone is running to St. Peter's Square.
The words: We Have a New Pope

are printed on the crawl
at the bottom of the TV screen
and the reporters seem shocked

because it happened so quickly.
But they have been waiting seventeen days,
seventeen very long days

between the death of John Paul II
and the election of this new one.
Now that they have seen the white smoke

imaginations willingly ponder
the likely and the unlikely,
the awaited 265th Pope.

Attesa Del Nuovo Papa!

Now the flags wave, and even though everyone
still misses the last one,
they watch as crimson draperies fold back,

open like hands to the world,
but suspense keeps them waiting.
Who can he be and what will they call him?

He once had an office down the hall,
a friendly face, smiles recall him as none other than

Cardinal Joseph Ratzinger,
now Pope Benedict XVI.
Viva il Papa!

And at last they hear the new Benedict's proclamation:

"After the great Pope John Paul II,
the cardinals have elected me—
a simple, humble worker in the vineyard
of the Lord. The fact that the Lord can
work with insufficient means consoles me,
and above all I entrust myself to your prayers,"

April 19, 2005

Rhineland

The news weightlessly transcends daylight
and white tassels swing

because the bell's toll was no longer somber. Now
sorrow turns her head toward the

divine pronouncement,
and inquisitively she dries her hands on a towel

of contentment while crowds run to Vatican Square,
where the illuminous dons the skullcap,

and processionals float balloons overhead.
Today the belated birthday gift of a rose

and a crosier comes to one Cardinal Ratzinger.
During this chronicle of the Eucharist, a pensive sky

is set ablaze, as if to say: "Carry on with spring."
This is a renaissance for the people.

It's no wonder
the Rhineland is jubilant.

Before and After

A Memory of Meeting the Pope

I.
He is kneeling at the foot of the altar
with his face toward the tabernacle.
You don't know how long he has been there

but when the chapel door opens
and you enter in front of your husband,
you see him praying there with his hands folded

as if pointing to the crucifix
and to the icon of the madonna,
away from his broad-shouldered humanness.

Dressed in his white papal cassock,
a tall and strong-looking man.
He doesn't move a muscle while there praying.
His physical size is dwarfed only by his holiness.

II.
Bishop Stanislaw Dziwisz
prepares the altar and helps the Holy Father vest.

Pope John Paul II is saying Holy Mass in Italian
when you notice for the first time a relief carved

in the marble behind the alter. St. Peter is hanging
upside-down, as if martyred before your very eyes.

The Polish nuns are singing, and their angelic voices
reach the stained-glass ceilings and soften the pain of

martyrdom.

For what seems like an eternity, you are caught up in
the eternal space of Holy Mass that goes on for

millennia.

On that day in the year 2000 AD, you kept notes
so you'd remember exactly what happened,

that your life changed forever (though you can't explain
why you're still so very much the same).

You still go to confession.

Saint Queen Jadwiga

The Polish Queen Jadwiga was crowned
October 16, 1384. A certain Polish priest,
Fr. Karol Wojtyla, celebrated a special Holy Mass
each year on the anniversary of her coronation.

Cardinal Wojtyla was elected to the Throne of Peter
October 16, 1978. He had prayed at the sarcophagus
of Queen Jadwiga before leaving for Rome. Silently, he
spoke her name when he became Pope John Paul II.

This poem was given to Pope John Paul II, in loving honor
of Queen Saint Jadwiga, on the twenty-sixth anniversary
of his election to the Chair of Peter, October 16, 2004.

Daughter of Poland,
To many others the crown was given;
First to Boleslas the Brave
And then to you it came tumbling.
What made a girl ready
For a king's crown?
One decade—that's all of life you knew.
How could your queen mother
Prepare you to be a king?
You had neither the height
Nor age to go to the university.
What would Kasimir the Great have said?
Poor, poor King Kasimir, the last of the Piasts;
He was in sore need of a son,
But neither God nor woman would give him one.
So upon his bed of pain, between his grandson

Kosko and nephew Louis of Anjou,
His Kingdom he split in twain, and then he died.
But Kosko died young, and then Louis died too!
(Poor Louis, known as Louis the no son,
Said his daughter Catherine would take the throne.
But she died before her father. Then Maria
Was to have the crown, but she became the queen
Of another kingdom. Oj! Oj!)
Yes, little Jadwiga, it is for you.
The king's crown is for your head.
You cannot play your make-believe.
Nor marry your charming childhood companion.
They say you screamed,

That you ran and hid in the cellar with the dried fish,
And you cried salt tears, for your youth was overing.
Jadwiga of Anjou, Jadwiga Princess,
Saint and girl, you emerged from the stores
With great generosity. And for a year
You were the King of Poland.
Soon Jagiello, your betrothed, the King of Lithuania,
Fought and saved your land from the Tartars;
Those Hordes choked for pleasure and took pretty girls.
Jagiello also set a brace against the Teutonic threat;
It would be good that you wed, they said.
You were twelve by then.
He was baptized on account of your faith,
Then you gave him your crown.
You stood beside him, co-ruler.

Mediator for the poor. Moderator for the diplomats.
Queen of love. Queen of Poland.
Traveling the land, you inspired warriors to peace,
And influenced lords against the enterprise of
Ambitiousness and folly. You renovated
Kasimir the Great's Krakow University
And assisted students from far and near.
You were a refuge from war.
What is this, they say?
Queen Jadwiga brings a child?
Alleluia Lithuania! Alleluia Poland!
The sand sifted slowly during
The time of confinement.
You screamed when the baby came.
You screamed, but the baby never cried.
And when the baby died, my sweet Queen,
You died too. Only twice as old as when
You were wed and two. You went to heaven
In thirteen ninety-nine.
What song can I sing for you?
What prayer can I say to comfort you,
My Saint, my Queen? What is this, they say?
Look to the throne of Peter?
Yes—there will sit a son for you.
And on the anniversary of your crowning, October sixteenth,
A son of Poland did rise to Peter's throne.
Today, sweet Saint Jadwiga, pray for our Pope
John Paul II. Tell him angels sing for him today.
Kiss him with a mother's love—today.

Prayer to the Queen of Poland

Who will be my mother now?

and who will be my friend?

Her dress is painted beatific blue
and is strewn with golden lilies.
Into her constant arms I run from dangers.

O keep me safe from all my fears,
from evil beings
and any other scary thing
that threatens to devour me.

Hide me behind your robes.
Cling to me, and I will lose myself
within your love.

Then your voice, your touch, your prophecy,
your holy womb, will bring me rest.

You, mother of my God, are also my mother.

For when you submitted to His birth,
ignoring the world and all its ways for love,
you did it for Him

and for me too.
And you would do it all again.

Blessed is the fruit of thy most holy womb.

O food and drink and lullaby so calm and safe.
You watched Him grow. You watched Him die.
Once a mother, always a mother.

Always my queen, listening, forgiving, consoling
Lady of Czestochowa, watch over us!

Fair Virgin

If chronicles could ease these modern woes,
then poems and pens would write truths into legends.
Or do we dare go back to a time
   to when dwellers
   told tales
   and traded things they'd borrowed?

There was a time, they say, and so I do believe
that a peasant man named Piast rose to the throne
of Poland.

In threes the Piast dynasty grew, son by son by son,
until the great prince Meiszko came to rule.
He was the fourth of the Piasts to reign.
   Though others say:
   Who knows?

But it was he, Meiszko, who brought his father's
dreams to pass, leading every tribe from Baltic
to Black Sea into solidarity. A remarkable man.

And truly Meiszko named these new lands Poland.

Ill was fate, and so too destiny, when it brought
with it an evil count who had been banished
by his Rhineland king,
   because of his evility.

This count named "Mad" waged war on Poland.
Not once, but twice he raised lance and sword.

Great battles Duke Meiszko led with gallant men
who fought and bled and died nobly
for victory—for their lord and the land.
　For chivalry.
　　Hear! Hear!
A toast to triumph over the scoundrel!

And to peaceful days and to Meiszko's bride-to-be,
Dubravka, a fair virgin who called love Christianity.
　And in love
　　she fell fast.

But before a wedding date was set,
this was the duchess' condition:
a Catholic baptism must be fixed upon his head,
which he did in nine hundred sixty-six.

It was by no coincidence, nor a surprise at all,
that this was when Poland entered written history.

And though some may have questioned the reason why
the duke and duchess gave the entire duchy
　　(that is all of Poland)
　　　to St. Peter's in Rome,

putting Poland directly under the protection
of the Pope Saint Sylvester. Most beg to differ
on that question.

About the rest of this story, there are volumes.

The Trumpeter

He was keeping watch in the bell tower,
unseen behind the brickstone walls,
waiting there inside the spire of Mary's church
in Krakow, across from market square.
    He was ready.

From crossbow slits, he looked
for hordes who might come to raid and make war.

By night or day, the sight of a Norde
or Tartar or Hun
would bring the trill,
calling men to ready be;
to fight the foe who dared,
or even contemplated
the wish to conquer Poland.

It was on that day before newdawn
that Mongols marched silently towards the gate,
an onslaught of more than five thousand men
with spears and swords.

At once he caught them in his sights
and set his horn to blast.

Long was the note that called to horse
and armored men to come to the barbican.
And long and grave and pure the sound
until, at once, the reveille fell silent.

A great lull came when an arrow
pierced the trumpeter's mighty throat.

A day of victory and sorrow
wherein many fought and died
for red and white and eagle's wings,
and freedom.

Remember this:
they died for a reason.

Did you hear it? Listen.
The trumpet sounds again.

From Conception

From that sacramental union came the gift
of offspring, created and given by God,
a unique human person from the beginning.

And he was—at that very instant—fully Karol Jozef Wojtyla,
the one to be born after nine months of waiting
to Mr. and Mrs. Karol and Emilia Wojtyla,
from that moment destined to be the actor,
the poet, the pope, a saint.

From inside the two-story apartment building a midwife watched
as the wings of dawn rose upon Wadowice, Poland.
Opening the window, she saw the puffs of white smoke
that were coming from the church across the street,
she heard the bells ring out the day of his birth.

The boy emerged with a booming voice,
a proclamation more than a cry—ah!
Ah, love life!

Lolek

"Do you think about me, Mamo?"

"Yes, my son. Constantly."

"Mamo, I hear your heart beating."

"It says, 'I love you, Lolek.'"

"What do you want from me, Mamo?"

"My son, you will do many great things."

"Like what, Mamo?"

"Maybe you will be a priest? Can you
 love this ocean of humanity?"

"Where are you going without me?"

"O Lolek, little lamb, from life to life."

"But I'm afraid. I'm afraid to be without you, Mamo."

"Love life, my son. But do not fear death.
 Do not crowd in line. When it's your turn,
 you will come and join me."

"O Mamo, how long? How long?"

"That's why life is a mystery, my son.
 You don't find out until the end."

Edmond

A big brother is someone who
is always there...

He is there the day you are born.
Your mother and I let him hold you
on that eighteenth day of May.

Years later, he ran up the apartment stairs
shouting: "Hey, Lolek! Let's play football!"
Do you remember that?
You were only ten. Now you are eleven—
almost a man yourself.

A man can live without his big brother.

Yes, it is tragic that your brother died
so soon after we lost your mother.
And, yes, the shadow of tragedy falls
on some when they are very young.

But sometimes one has to wonder
what you would become without it.
There is destiny and reasonability
and faith that God has a plan here.

For you Wadowice isn't like it used to be.
Our Lady of Perpetual Help Church
is still across the street, but you won't hear
Edmond coming up the stairs to visit.

Yes, I know you hate scarlet fever
because that's what he died of...

Come on, son. Let's go have pierogi
at Alojzy Banas' restaurant.
You can wear this old army coat of mine.
Get some green thread from Mama's sewing box.
I'll make it fit you perfectly.

My Father

was often on his knees late into the night.
He was a soldier, and death was no stranger to him.
But I was only a boy then, not a man...and after
my brother Edmond died, my father was all I had left;
his words were my only comfort.

Don't be sad, Karol.
Your mother and your brother
and your sister are in heaven.

Karol, have you finished your studies?
Have you said your prayers?
Let's roll up the rug and play indoor soccer.
Yes—your mother is watching us...
but she won't mind too much.

Karol? Would you like to serve at Holy Mass?
You'd also like to be an actor in a play? That's fine.
Read, my son. Read books and poems and scripts.
Put them to memory.

Have you said your prayers, Karol?
Can you tell me the complete history of Poland?
Did I ever tell you about the time when your mother and I...

How about we roll up the rug and play soccer?
You don't want to play soccer? You have work to do?
You want to be a poet? a playwright? an actor?

Ah yes, my son, you must discover for yourself
what God has planned for you. Do whatever you do well
and do it for Him. Search deeply your dreams.
It is already there, like a memory. You must find it, my son.

Read books and write them if you wish.
And study hard in every subject.
But, Karol, never forget to say your prayers.

When I found you there, my father, my captain, I cried.
You died while I was working in the limestone quarry.
Under the brutal Nazi occupation, you had grown old and ill.
On my knees beside your body I wept because...

I should have been there...I should have done more for you.

"Please, Papa! Don't go!
I beg you. Don't leave me behind.
Stay with me just one more day.
For my very blood is vanishing into the vault
of eternal loneliness," I cried.

Now when I am on my knees late into the night,
I feel close to my father.

O earth. O dramatic stage. O life. O poem.
What can I give You in return, my God,
for having given me the gift of a good father?

I shall let God decide whether and when
I am left with only my pen.

Endings

Notes on Suffering

Notes based on the Apostolic Letter
on the Christian meaning of Suffering
by Pope John Paul II: Salvifici Doloris

(and here, with all-unable pen, I attempt to summarize
and in some cases analyze, if not grasp fully, then in part,
the meaning of suffering).

The world of human suffering is groaning
for another world—a world of love.

And so the apostle Paul wrote to the Romans:
"I rejoice in my sufferings for your sake."

The experience is a universal one,
speaking here of what is essential
to the nature of man's suffering;
something wider than sickness,
taking on infinite forms and types,
psychological, physical, and moral...

just study the examples that include
but are not limited to the times when persons
are deprived of human love and compassion,
surrounded by danger, depleted of hope;
when their lives and livelihoods are tossed by
the waves of a flood, an earthquake, the violence of war;
when one faces the reality of one's limits,
faces one's own death,
which we all inevitably do—
all these are forms of agony.

And it is perfectly human to wonder why.
To wonder—if existence is good
where does the bitter pain fit in?
How could it come from God
when God is all perfect, pure and good?

There is free will.
Free will: the fact that a person can choose
to do good deeds or harmful deeds.

Then there are random natural disasters,
tortures by machine, accidental happenings,

mysterious miseries that are not caused
by any fault or action of the sufferer or of another.

There are mysteries here,
more than meets the eye,
but it does appear that free will and organic possibilities
belong to the earth, to creatures and created things.

Ah, existence, albeit good, begs the question: Why?

This is a question that an animal would never ask:
What does it mean when I suffer?
Whether I suffer alone or with others?
And why can I not avoid pain or avoid wondering why?

Some other questions are:
Does God allow a Satan to vex us?
Could it be said that free will and randomness
bring us together
and create in us the need for,
even the longing for, the Divine Creator?

And what, then, is evil?
A Lucifer choosing to turn away from God.

There are mysteries here.

And so, Job asked God: Why?
We all know the story.
Job was a good man, innocent,
but he lost everything.
It was not because he was evil.
He was compassionate.

When he prayed for his enemies,
Job foreshadowed the messianic mission:
to conquer suffering through love.

Here is where we too enter into and discover
the answer to the "why" of suffering,
if we look to divine mercy and love.
And it was in the days of King Herod
that this Jesus of Nazareth was born.

During the reign of Tiberius Caesar
this Jesus took upon himself the suffering
of the world, not depriving Himself of humanity,
though innocent, though divine,
delivering himself up to death,
transcending earthly pain with Love,
annihilating evil at its root,
creating the Path into this Mystery
on *Via Dolorosa*—
the source of divine love
that accomplished the definitive
work of salvation.

Here is where the meaning of suffering
changed for all eternity;
transforming disillusionment into hope,
even though His death did not abolish
the existence of suffering in the world,
there is a new atmosphere in the midst
of human affliction,
a message of Love for all humankind,
rendering enormous deliverance.

And for those whose experience is united with this hope,
even their own suffering, caught up with His, is redemptive.
(This is why St. Paul rejoiced in his chains of imprisonment,
because he believed his suffering would:
"Complete what was lacking in Christ's afflictions.")

On the path of *Salvifici Doloris*
we, too, enter into the Paschal Mystery
and into its meaning of love,
embracing all humanity,
offering prayers for the world.

Like the Good Samaritan,
together with Mary and all of the Saints,
we draw on this infinite source of redemption.

And this is the Christian answer to the inevitable question:
What is the meaning of suffering?

Endings

1.

Remember that May when bullets came,
that day when he awoke from surgery
and wrote down on a sheet of paper:

"I am still Totus Tuus."

Call it the Month of May if you wish,
but don't forget it's all for Virgin Mary;
Dawn's Gate knows all about endings.

For the love of your brethren and friends,
gaze upon forgiveness.
And remember, too, the fourth month—April.

2.

It was Holy Week when
he returned to the upper room,
calling with silence, struck with fever.

Gladly we went there with him.
We needed no special invitation.
Returning to the Cenacle after
having never been there before,
we waited for his voice.

Cover me with the purple robe of this passion.
I embrace the cross that is within my body.

The procession around the coliseum,
where I am not, is now the portal
to another world.

How my blood and bone and very flesh
seem to breathe for their sake.

Yet this is not my last.
This is not yet the end.

3.
There are luminous clouds overhead,
the color of melons,
like the fruits in Tsarkova's *Last Supper,*
like her face,
soft against his hand
in that photograph before Easter.

4.
It was Wednesday.
That was the last time we saw him.
Glorious are those goodbyes of 11:00 a.m.
Farewell first Wednesday of Easter,
never to return again.

5.
I have searched for you, and now you have come to me.

There are pilgrims outside my window.
What are they singing?

I was dreaming about my mother again.
It was Friday and she was fasting from meat.
From the kitchen came the smell of home cooking.
It was something sweet like *babka swiateczna,*
but it was only a dream.

What are the people chanting?
I hear the multitude of melodies.
And it sounds just like Youth Day.

The world is at your window my Pope, my friend.
They are singing Hosanna in the Highest
like a choir of cherubim.
But don't you think you should rest?

Let them stay. Let them parade in the streets.
Let them sing me to sleep.
I can almost see through the stained-glass window now.

But who is going to plant the sapling
where the Russian olive tree didn't grow?
And what about the lavender hedge
that has grown too tall?
We can let it take over.
There is a gardener, isn't there?
You must find him.

6.
Inside the Vatican an Archbishop is saying Holy Mass,
a Vigil, the Feast of Divine Mercy.

Holy viaticum anoint my head with oil.
O Divine Piazza welcome me.

A priest is saying: "This is my body...This is my blood."

The Saints have now filled my room
and they are saying the Lord's Prayer.
The Sacrifice of the Mass
is offered here on earth and
it leads me to a world without end.

7.
Whose joy is touching the windowpane?

Saint Faustina Kowalska,
Blessed Mother Theresa,
Sister Lucia.

There will be no one standing at the window
to greet the faithful tomorrow,
no one at all.

8.
In closing his last will and testament
Pope John Paul II wrote:
    To all I want to say just one thing:
    May God reward you!
    In manus tuas, Domine, commendo spiritum meun
    (Into your hands, Lord, I commend my spirit).

His final words during this earthly life:
  "Let me go to the Father's house."

******

Saint Pope John Paul II was a voice of peace and morality for the entire world.

On April 2, 2005, he passed from this earthly life surrounded by friends. He was beatified on Sunday, May 1, 2011. On April 27, 2014, he was canonized a saint.

Acknowledgments

I am grateful to the editors of *Zeszyty Karmelitanskie,* where five of these poems, earlier versions translated into Polish, were published. Thanks to Agnieszka Laska for translating my poems. I am grateful, too, to the editors of the *Catholic Sentinel,* where "When the Pope Dies" and "Zinc and Wood" appeared.

A special thanks to my poetry editor, Vinnie Kinsella. Thank you to both Holly Franko for editorial help and to Jennifer Omner for helping bring this collection of poems to publication. And I render a very special thanks to Michael Hamilton for stepping in to design the book cover.

Above all, I thank my wonderful husband, Greg Hamilton, for his infinite support and his patience.

www.ingramcontent.com/pod-product-compliance
Lightning Source LLC
Chambersburg PA
CBHW031323040426
42443CB00005B/197